THE IMPORTANCE
OF FAITH
IN COUNSELING

Jay E. Adams

Institute for Nouthetic Studies, a ministry of Mid-America Baptist Theological Seminary, 2095 Appling Road, Memphis, TN 38016mabts. edu / nouthetic.org / INSBookstore.com

Importance of Faith in Couseling by Jay E. Adams
Copyright © 2021 by the Institute for Nouthetic Studies,
© 2007 by Jay E. Adams

ISBN: 978-1-949737-36-3 (Print)
ISBN: 978-1-949737-37-0 (eBook)
Old ISBN: 978-1-889032-58-0

Editor: Donn R. Arms
Design: James Wendorf | www.FaithfulLifePublishers.com

Library of Congress Cataloging-in-Publication Data Names: Adams, Jay E., 1929 - 2020

Title: Importance of Faith in Counseling / Jay E. Adams

Description: Memphis: Institute for Nouthetic Studies, 2021 Identifiers: ISBN 9781949737363 (paper) Classification: LCC BV4012.2.A435 | DDC 253.5

Published in the United States of America

Table of Contents

Introduction

"Without faith it is impossible to please Him." That is the principle that the divinely moved biblical writer laid down (Hebrews 11:6). That principle is absolute and wide-reaching in scope and application. It was true in Old Testament times and it is still true today. Contrary to those who thought that intellectualism, ceremonies, or good works have merit in and of themselves, the Bible is as clear as it could be that these ideas are false. Those proud academicians, the so-called Doctors of the Law, knew the Scriptures inside out. They could quote large portions of the Old Testament from memory. And they even knew of the prediction of the coming Savior,[1] but their knowledge could not save them because they lacked faith. For all of their intellectual prowess, they were ignorant of the way of salvation, as Jesus' conversation with Nicodemus revealed (John 3:10). Intellectualism is not pleasing to God.

Nor do ceremonies suffice. The Jews were proud of their circumcision, which was intended to mark them as (not make them) the people of God. Paul wrote, "Circumcision is nothing and uncircumcision is nothing" (1 Corinthians 7:19). And God declared that He is pleased only where there is circumcision of the heart (Jeremiah 4:4). This too comes through faith.

And finally, it is utterly clear that God is not interested in all of the works a man might do. The story of the Rich Young Ruler

---

1 Indeed, they were able to tell Herod the place of the Christ's birth (Matthew 2:5).

makes that plain, as do the words of Isaiah to apostate Israel (Isaiah 54:4) and Paul's declaration that salvation is not "from works" (Ephesians 2:9).

There is no doubt that knowledge, ceremonies, and "good" works are meaningless without faith. It is only when they grow out of faith, an exhibition of it, that they are pleasing to God.

Ever since the fall of Adam, man's problem always has been the attempt to please God without faith. And what is true of many aspects of life is certainly true of counseling. That is why I have written this book. I am concerned that the Christian counselor might attempt to help others without considering the importance of faith. Suffice it to say, faith must permeate every aspect of the counseling process.

In this book I shall examine various aspects of biblical counseling to delineate the place of faith in each. If you think that you do not need to be told about this matter, then please skim through this book and notice the many areas that, if you are like many, you may not have noticed. I think that even if you are conscious of the importance of faith, you may discover much that you will find helpful in bringing your counselees to faith. If they—or you—set forth on any endeavor without faith, it will fail. Outwardly, there may be temporal success, but true success is doing that which pleases God. And remember, without faith it is impossible to please Him.

1

A Summary Look at Faith

Three aspects of faith describe what God is talking about in the Bible. They are *Understanding* of His truth; *Agreement* with its content; *Dependence* upon His Word. Let's consider each.

Understanding

During the Second World War, a widely-distributed poster pictured a soldier administering blood plasma to a wounded companion out on the battlefield. It was a well drawn and in many ways a moving scene. Under the picture on the poster were the words: KEEP THE FAITH. It is those words that, doubtless well meant, lead me to mention it. "*The* faith?" What faith? Faith in what? There was no content to these words and, consequently, they were meaningless. When many speak of "Having faith in God" or in "His promises," they may be nearly as vague. What God? What promises? To whom were they made? In response to what? It is this sort of indefiniteness that characterizes a television commercial currently run by the United Methodist Church. In it are phrases that laud "openness": "open minds, open hearts, open doors."[1] Open to what? To whom? For what reasons?

Plainly, biblical counselors must have a much clearer view of that which God calls them and their counselees to place faith in. What could be more important than knowing God's truth? How

---

1 What a sad commentary on a denomination! There is no mention of Jesus Christ, the Bible—or even God! The church's message is openness to any and all views and all comers!

can one place faith in what he does not know? That is why the first aspect of biblical faith must always be "understanding." God's truth has content. It is not vague and amorphous. It is a body of teaching including truth about God, the gospel of salvation, and directions for living the Christian life. And, lest these teachings become distorted through transmission by word of mouth, they were recorded in a Book of books: the Bible (preeminently in the Gospels and epistles of the New Testament). The Christian church has no right to alter, add, or abridge what God has supernaturally caused to be recorded in these books. The content was delivered to plain, ordinary people, clearly set forth and, as a result, is understandable. There is no excuse for uncertainty.

Agreement

The second aspect of biblical faith is "agreement." Having understood what God says, the one who exercises genuine faith agrees with what he reads in the Scriptures. The word for agreement used throughout the New Testament is *homologeo*, which means "to say the same thing." It is used in the papyri to describe business agreements. It is the term from which we obtain our words "Confession of Faith." A confession of faith is a doctrinal statement accepted by a group of people, all of whom declare that they are in agreement with it. To "confess Christ" is to agree with what God says about Him and His work.[2] There can be no true, acceptable faith apart from agreement with God's Word.

Dependence

Faith in the biblical sense is not mere understanding and agreement; it also requires trust (or "dependence") upon what God has said. It is a staking of one's future upon the truth of His Word. This aspect of faith requires one to depend upon what God has said

---

2 Confession of sin is agreement with what God says about one's sin and application to one's own attitudes and behavior.

concerning Himself and His plan of redemption. Such dependence, in the first place, means trusting in a Savior Who according to the Scriptures died for sinners and rose from the dead. It is that truth upon which God's elect people trust for time and eternity. Then, having trusted Christ as one's Savior, the Christian must depend upon Him and His Word for wisdom to live thereafter in ways pleasing to God.

Three in One

Having discussed the three aspects of genuine faith, let me hasten to say that faith is not to be divided. These are *aspects* of one thing, not separate elements. Without all three, "faith" (whatever it may be) is not biblical faith. Understanding alone does not save or sanctify. Agreement, in addition, is not enough. There must also be a wholehearted dependence as well. That is why the apostles said one must "believe *on* the Lord Jesus Christ" (Acts 16:31).

I shall visit these three aspects of true faith again and again from one angle or another as we proceed. It is important, therefore, to get a grasp of that which faith consists of before discussing its various relations to counseling.

Faith and the Future

Faith has one eye fixed on the future, and this affects the way that the other eye views the present. In Matthew 6:19–21, Jesus tells his disciples that they should lay up treasures in heaven. He also explains that wherever one's treasure is, there his heart will be also. It is clear, then, that Jesus thought that His own should look forward to the eternal reward rather than to strive only for those rewards which may be found in this life. The writer of Hebrews spells this out in no uncertain terms when, in speaking of the heroes of faith, he writes, "they desire a better (that is, a heavenly) country" (Hebrews 11:16). No wonder that he wrote, "Now faith is a solidly grounded certainty about what we hope for, a conviction about the reality of things we don't see" (v. 1). Faith always has this component of trusting in God's Word, whether it has to do with that which takes place in this life or in the life to come, in face of the fact that it has not yet taken place. As this verse says, it has to do with hope. Hope, in the Scriptures, is not the hope-so hope that we talk about. It is the expectation of God's fulfillment of His promises. It is faith that assures us of the certainty of them.

2

The Proper Mix

The writer of Hebrews, who spoke so much about faith, had this to say:

Indeed, the good news came to us just as it did to them; nevertheless, the word that they heard was of no benefit to them because it wasn't mixed with faith by those who heard it (Hebrews 4:2).

The word "mixed" has in it the idea of compounding things together.[1] The "good news" does not in itself transform people. As it is proclaimed, it must be met and mingled with faith. In Romans 10, where Paul discusses the importance of preaching, he also speaks of the "word of faith which we are preaching" (v. 8). Here, we see him saying the same thing: the word (message) that must be met and mingled with faith.

"OK," you say, "but all of that has to do with salvation. We know that one is saved by faith and not by works. This book is supposed to deal with faith in biblical counseling. You must show that faith is of importance to counseling as it is to justification."

---

1 In 1 Corinthians 12:24—the only other place where the word is used in the New Testament—the meaning is clearly "combined" or "composed of." The members of the body are to work in sync with one another. However one translates, the writer's idea is to show how two or more elements work together to bring about something else (here, a "body" of people thought of as one).

Faith In Sanctification

Fair enough. In Thessalonians, Paul speaks of "remembering your work that comes from faith" (1 Thessalonians 1:3). Here, as he and James always do, Paul sees works—that is, works that please God—flowing from faith. Indeed, when you look at the accomplishments of the Old Testament saints listed in Hebrews, the works they did for God were all done "by faith." The writer rings the changes on that short phrase. Since in counseling we want people to put off their old unrighteous ways by putting on new righteous ones, it is clear that if these new ways are to please God, they must be the products of faith. But notice it is not faith alone that brings about the desired result. This faith is faith in God's truth; not faith in the abstract. So, once more we see how faith, met and mingled with truth, produces that with which God is pleased.

Let's look briefly at how this works out in counseling. Consider the following slice of a counseling case.

A Case of Unbelief

"I simply can't do what you are asking, Pastor. I've tried and tried again, but I fail every time. I've forgiven him, but I don't think it's possible to stop thinking all the time about her in my husband's arms!"

Well, Martha, I know it's difficult, but if you believe and do what God says, you *will* be able to do it. Remember, forgiveness means that you have promised not to bring the matter up to Tom, to others, or to yourself. When God forgives, He promises, "For I will forgive their wrongdoing and never again remember their sin" (Jer. 31:34, HCS²B). And, according to Ephesians 4:32, your forgiveness of others must be based on God's forgiveness of your sins.[3]

---

2 HCSB Holman Christian Standard Bible
3 For explicit details about biblical forgiveness, see my book *From Forgiven to Forgiving.*

"I've read all of the passages that you mentioned over and over, but I think that it's simply impossible for me to do it."

Instead of sitting around thinking about Tom's offense, if you would get to work and fulfill your daily responsibilities, you would begin to get your mind off the sin and on to more wholesome God-honoring matters. And there are other things that are involved in your promise ...

"I know, but I still don't believe what you say is possible."

Wait a minute. Do you think that it's what I am saying about forgiving that is impossible—or what God is saying?

"Both. I don't believe God expects me not to bring the matter up to myself any more. I've prayed and prayed for God to remove the heartache, but He doesn't answer me."

Well, now I think that I see what your problem is. It isn't a matter of God's way of forgiveness that is a failure; rather, you are failing because you don't truly believe that what God says is possible. And you doubt that God will help you.

"Right."

Then, let's talk first about your disbelief. We will get nowhere until that matter is settled. James says that the doubter "shouldn't suppose that he will receive anything from the Lord" (1:6–8). You see, God's truth must be mixed with faith. It's something like adding the ingredients that, when combined, produce an effect that neither will produce when alone. Your prayers are ineffectual because they are not mixed with faith. Listen to Hebrews 4:2....

A Priority over Procedure

In this exchange, the pastor temporarily revised his counseling plan so as to deal with Martha's doubt. When he recognized that it was her lack of faith that was getting in the way of progress, he understood that counseling would not be effectual until that problem was rectified.

So, without question, it is crucial to look for possible absence of faith when you discover that the promises of God are not taking place. If she had done as the pastor was trying to tell her—to stop sitting idly bringing up the sin to herself, to fix her mind on acceptable themes mentioned in Philippians 4, and so on— she would begin to get the peace of God she was seeking.[4] But lack of faith, not some unattainable nature of God's truth, was her fundamental problem.[5] And until resolved, it would continue to cause her prayers to be unanswered. He, therefore, must first spend time helping Martha to gain the faith that she needs to enter into cooperative, faithful agreement with the Word of God.

So, faith is essential to achieving anything that God commands you to do. Attempts to please God that are made apart from faith become like the works of the scribes and the Pharisees; they are "dead works" (Hebrews 6:1; 9:14). They are dead because the scribes and pharisees lack the faith that gives life to their works. Never proceed in counseling when you are working with a counselee who doubts God's Word. That matter takes such priority that (as in the example above) all other matters should be laid aside, and lack of faith in God's promises should become the new counseling problem.

---

4   But in general, of course, counselees should not primarily seek "peace" or relief. They should seek to obey God whether the relief they wish comes or not.

5   When Paul writes of saving faith in Romans 10:6ff., he notes that "the righteousness that is by faith" should not have to be sought in places impossible to reach (such as heaven or the abyss). Instead, he declares, "The word is near to you, in your mouth and in your heart (that is, the word of faith that we are preaching)" (v. 8). The same is true of faith leading to the sanctification of believers. The promises of God are not unattainable; they are as close as the message you hear. God's promises are readily understood and easily entered into by faith!

3

Making a Point of Faith

Many counselees will attempt to do God's work apart from faith, thus robbing it of spiritual life (the Spirit produces His fruit where there is faith). Because of this, prior to giving any homework assignment,[1] it is wise to *stress* that the counselee must enter into the effort in faith. Explain briefly to counselees that it is impossible to please God apart from faith. Most will come to see you without the slightest thought about the matter. Yet, in spite of your encouragement (and warning) some counselees will pay little heed. They will plunge ahead, in their own wisdom and strength, failing to recognize that faith is essential. As we have seen, in part, faith is dependence. Just as one depends upon Jesus Christ for justification, so he must also depend upon the Spirit for wisdom and strength (cf. Galatians 3:1–3). Works of righteousness must be done in dependence upon God, not upon one's self.

Perhaps one of the most useful verses that stresses this fact is Philippians 2:13: "It is God Who is producing in you both the willingness and the ability to do the things that please Him." You probably will find yourself referring to it frequently. The willingness to endure in the face of difficulty and trial is initiated and sustained by faith. A proper recognition of the fact that one is frail[2] and helpless in himself will cause him to cry out to God in faith for the

---

1 For details about homework in counseling, see *The Christian Counselor's Manual.*
2 One of the Hebrew words for "man" is *anosh,* which means "sick or frail man."

ability to achieve His purposes. So, faith is not only desirable, it is crucial.

An Atmosphere of Belief

In the first counseling session, you will want to create a pervasive biblical atmosphere.[3] Part of fostering that atmosphere is making it clear to the counselee that it is God, not the counselor, with Whom the counselee primarily has to do. The counselor is simply a minister of the Word who encourages his counselee to obey God's commands found in His Word. The Israelites at Sinai promised to do all that God commanded, and again and again failed to keep their promise. This was because they did not depend upon Him for wisdom and strength. Why was that? We are told that "they weren't able to enter in because of *unbelief*" (Hebrews 3:19 [italics mine]). You want your counselee to depend upon God to enable him to bring about the changes that He desires. That dependence, as we saw earlier, is an aspect of faith.

No Quietism

Dependence on God, however, is not some sort of substitute for obedience. The Bible does not teach quietism[4] in the Bible. Rather, faith is the dynamic through which the power of God is tapped by the believer *so as to* obey. By faith the believer does what God requires in *His* strength. He must obey. Neither is faith a substitute for obedience. True faith is intimately connected to obedience, as we shall see later on.

Now, in discussing faith with a counselee, you must make it clear that you are not necessarily challenging his faith. Let him know how important the matter is and that is why you are emphasizing it. If he says that he isn't sure about his faith in God's promises,

---

3 For more about this, see *Three Crucial Stages of Biblical Counseling.*
4 The view that God does the work for His children, instead of them.

it will be necessary for you to bring everything to a halt and deal with this matter.[5] In other words, you will not knowingly allow a counselee to blunder ahead, depending upon his own resources rather than placing his faith in God. If you fail to show concern about the matter of faith in counseling, then you may be leading many counselees into dead works. These do not satisfy God or, in the long run, the counselee himself. You must be careful, then, not to allow counselees to think that they have the ability or wisdom to fulfill God's Word apart from faith. Otherwise you will deceive them and, what is worse, misrepresent God. Too many counselees think that they are doing that which pleases God, when all they are doing is pleasing the counselor, their spouse, or someone else. Because this is such a fundamental matter, you must never overlook it.

How often do you ask a counselee, "Do you believe that God will do this for you?" And, if you receive an uncertain or negative answer, do you go on to say, "Then we can't proceed further until your doubts are cleared up"? At that point when you discover his lack of faith, you should explain and apply Hebrews 4:2.

Seeing Faith at Work

It is, however, not possible for you to look into a counselee's heart to determine whether or not he has faith.[6] That is between

---

5 I shall discuss how to do so later on.

6 In Acts 14:9 Luke wrote, "He [a cripple] listened to Paul as he spoke. Paul looked straight at him and saw that he had faith to be healed." Then, Paul healed him. At first, this verse may seem to contradict verses like 1 Samuel 16:7 where we are told that man looks only on the outward appearance but God looks on the heart (see also 2 Chron. 6:30). There is no contradiction. Notice, the fact of *seeing* is emphasized: "Paul looked straight at him and saw ..." What he saw, we are not told, but that it was something external in how the man responded to Paul's preaching is certain. Certainly, this response was obvious enough that it impressed Paul with his faith.

him and God. By his actions and words, you may suspect that he does not have faith. Whenever these may *seem* to indicate that he lacks faith in the endeavor he is setting out to fulfill during the forthcoming week, you may want to stop him, explain how faith is necessary to accomplish the task, and ask him if he has such faith.

At any rate, in this chapter, my whole purpose is to do exactly what I hope you will do for your counselees—make a point of the importance of faith.

4

How Much Faith Does It Take?

The disciples protested to Jesus that they needed more faith to obey His commands about forgiveness: "Then the apostles said to the Lord, 'Increase our faith!' " (Luke 17:5). In response, He made it clear that even a smidgen of faith is enough to do wonders: "If you have faith like a mustard seed, you could say to this mulberry tree, 'Be uprooted and be planted in the sea,' and it would obey you" (v. 6). On this occasion, Jesus was resisting the apostles' excuses by explaining that they did not need more faith; what they needed was obedience (cf. v. 10). There are times when a counselee will protest that he simply doesn't have enough faith to do some difficult thing that God requires of him. On those occasions, like their Lord, counselors must distinguish between a true lack and an excuse. In the passage just referred to Jesus used powerful hyperbole to dislodge such seemingly pious dodges. Be sure that you have such a response safely stored in your counseling arsenal and ready at hand for use.

You may ask, "But aren't there other passages where Jesus complained about the apostles' lack of faith? And, what about the person who approached Him saying, 'I believe,' but then added, 'help my unbelief?' "

These are two important matters to consider when thinking about the *amount* of faith a person may or may not have.

Some Have Little Faith

To begin with, you must not think that there is any sort of contradiction between the Luke 17 passage and those that we are now about to consider. There isn't. Keep in mind that in Luke, the apostles were making an excuse. The fact is that they *did* have enough faith. They believed that what He said was true; they simply didn't want to do it. Jesus' withering reply made that plain. Their problem was lack of obedience (cf. v. 10). In the other instances that we shall now take a look at, the situation is entirely different.

First, consider Jesus' rebuke in Matthew 6:30: "You have so little faith!" Jesus was commenting on the worry that He discerned in the lives of those to whom He was speaking. They were concerned about food and clothing when they should have been seeking the kingdom of God and His righteousness. Worry eroded and threatened to replace faith. Also, in Matthew 8:26 we read, "Why are you afraid, you men of little faith?" Again, in Matthew 14:31 we read that Jesus said to Peter, "Little-faith, why did you doubt?"

In these three citations one thing seems apparent: in each case, those Jesus addressed were either afraid or worried (which is a milder form of fear). Fear is an obstacle to faith. When a counselee is afraid to follow Jesus' commands, his faith diminishes. Notice how Jesus speaks of their small faith, even calling Peter by the nickname "Little-Faith." Faith will wane as fear waxes. The two are antithetical. So, in order to overcome fear, one must believe, trusting himself to Jesus and His Word. In order to eliminate doubt, like Abraham, who didn't know where God was sending him or what he was to do when he got there, the counselee must venture forth believing that God knows what is best for him. Fear of the known or of the unknown paralyzes faith if it is allowed to do so. The believer, in prayer, must ask God to help as he goes forth, however hesitatingly, to fulfil God's commands.

Faith Fortifies

In contrast to weak (or small) faith, there are a number of passages in which God's servants are said to be "full of faith" (cf. Acts 6:5; 11:24). About Abraham, it is written that his faith "didn't weaken" (Romans 4:19), and that he "didn't hesitate about God's promise because of unbelief, but fortified by faith, he gave God the glory" (v. 20). Indeed, rather than be weakened by doubt, he accepted God's promise about a son in circumstances that seemed to make its fulfillment nearly impossible. And he was able to do so, notice carefully, because his faith *fortified* him. Now, that is the important thing to teach counselees who may have little faith. Don't let them hesitate in unbelief, but tell them to go forward fulfilling the tasks God has given them, fortified by faith.

Help Is Available

Now, what about the man who doubted, but wanted to believe (Mark 9:24)? He asked Jesus for "help" to rid himself of the unbelief that was threatening to crowd out the minimal amount of faith that he had. Two facts in this account protrude: (1) the man acknowledged his struggle with unbelief and (2) he came to the right person for help to rid himself of it. That is a marvelous passage to use when counselees struggle with unbelief. Of course, the struggle must always be one in which the person genuinely wants to believe, though he may still retain nagging doubts about God's promises. You must urge him to find his help in Jesus Christ. How? By prayerfully asking the Spirit to help him as he studies the Scriptures concerning his counseling difficulty.

Faith Can Be Increased

So, it is apparent that while some have more faith than others, and that no Christian may excuse himself from fulfilling God's requirements by saying that his faith is too small, it is desirable to increase faith. Jesus wants His people to grow; and one of those ways in which growth must take place is in faith. The need for a mix of faith and works is most striking on the occasion when we read that because of the town's "unbelief," Jesus "couldn't do any miracles" in Nazareth (Mark 6:6, 7). Should *we* expect great responses from counselees who evidence nothing but unbelief?

Well then, how much faith does it take to please God? Certainly, He is displeased with our doubts and lack of faith. He rebukes unbelief whenever it occurs. But even "mustard seed" faith can lead to wondrous results among those who obey in faith. As one grows spiritually, his faith will increase, and as his faith increases, he will grow even more spiritually. How may he become more and more trusting? By confessing his lack of faith and asking Jesus for help. As he reads about the saints who exhibited wholehearted faith, his own faith will grow. That crowd of Old Testament witnesses (Heb. 12:1) to what God can do through faith should encourage, enlighten, and motivate a counselee to act in faith. Assign counselees to make a thorough study of Hebrews 11. And, as we see others today who have faith that brings God-pleasing results, we should "imitate their faith" (Hebrews 13:7). The writer says to "take a look at the results of their behavior." God promised, they obeyed in faith, God blessed.

"How much faith is necessary?" Your Christian counselee must have faith equal to the task before him. And he must never say that God has called him to do that which he cannot have the faith to accomplish. As he steps forth with whatever faith he has, he will recognize that his faith grows. In James 1:25, the writer tells us that a person is blessed "in the doing" (not before). And, it was James who also taught us that God "gives greater help" to the humble (James 4:6).[1] May He use your biblical counseling to bring that help to many!

---

1 Humility is essential to true faith. This is clear since faith requires dependence upon Another while acknowledging that one's own ability is inadequate for a task.

5

Understanding, Accepting, and Doing God's Will

The Three Are One

Previously, we looked at three aspects of faith in a purely analytical manner. We shall now consider their practical outworking. The interesting fact is that each one requires the others to become fruitful. That means that in their practical outworking, they are inseparable. It is only when you look at them analytically that you may differentiate each from the others as an aspect of faith.

Take *understanding* for instance. Understanding the gospel message that Christ died for our sins and rose from the dead (1 Corinthians 15:3, 4) is necessary for saving faith. And that same understanding is necessary for *agreement* (acceptance of the message and the One about Whom it speaks). Those who understand and agree trust Christ—or there is no true agreement. But the natural man has no such ability. In 1 Corinthians 2, Paul shows how he can neither hear, see, nor believe in his heart because he cannot understand the things of the Spirit of God. That is because those things must be *understood* spiritually. That is to say, they must be understood as the Spirit enables one to do so. They make no sense to the unbeliever; they are foolishness to him. He cannot understand how trusting one's self for eternity to "a so-called Savior" Who lived so long ago can do anything for him. To the unbeliever, it simply doesn't make sense. So he rejects Him.

In addition, look at *agreement*. Suppose one can understand what the message is (i.e., its content; not its meaning for himself) and why others think that they can be saved by believing in it, but he cannot agree with its content. He will scorn anyone who would stake his life and eternity upon such a message. He can not and will not agree to the truth because he is spiritually blind. To him, the Bible seems a dead book when the real problem is that he is dead to it! Thus, there can be no agreement.

And he will not *trust* Christ as Savior because though he understands and knows that he should agree to it if it is true, because of unbelief he refuses to *depend* on it. He will not stake eternity upon the gospel. In other words, the unbelieving heart has problems with every aspect of faith. That is why, as Paul says, "Those who are in the flesh cannot please God" (Romans 8:8). Unless he is regenerated, he will not believe.

Lingering Unbelief

Now, what has that to do with counseling believers? A counselee may have been converted, but he is far from perfect. He brings into the new life many of the old ways he developed in the former one. Those patterns of life include his ways of thinking as well as attitudes and actions. That means that unbelief in God and His Word still crops up when God's commands are given to him. Like Thomas, he may find it difficult to shake off patterns of skepticism and unbelief. He still often doubts, hesitates, and even resists. He must learn to put off these patterns from the past and substitute new patterns that are in harmony with God's revealed will. It is precisely because he fails to believe that he gets into trouble. That is why in every act of disobedience, if you look for it, you will find an element of disbelief. When he cannot find his way out of some difficulty, then, he may come for counseling. When he does, what must the counselor do?

After the Battle

Obviously, when a counselor faces one who is caught up in sinful patterns of thought which get in the way of belief, he must deal with it. Paul discusses this in 2 Corinthians 10:3–6. Here, he pictures the battle for the minds of men as a warfare fought with spiritual weapons. The strongholds that men rear up are no match for these divinely powerful weapons. That should encourage you. They tear down arguments raised against the truth and take every thought captive for Jesus Christ. Now, although a prisoner surrenders to Christ as Savior, not every faithless thought is thereby subdued. Many doubts and fears remain. Unbelief lurks in various corners of his heart.

These matters of unbelief manifest themselves in actions. Indeed, Paul acknowledged this when he wrote that he was "prepared also to deal justly with every act of disobedience, after your obedience is complete" (v. 6). That means there is a lot of work to do in a convert's thought life *after* conversion. That work includes dealing with persistent disobedience in the form of doubting and unbelief. It is in this theatre of the war—the mopping up work after the initial victory—that counselors find themselves doing battle.

As Paul says, the task, in this regard, is to "deal justly with every act of disobedience." That is where counseling comes in. Notice, he does not say that Christ's prisoners ought to be treated unkindly, as the modern-day Iraqis often do. They are to be treated "justly." That means they are to be helped according to the severity (or lack of it) that the disbelief requires. Clearly, counselors, who are among those who engage in such work, must be careful to do so "justly." They must learn how to strongly rebuke and reprove when necessary, and to encourage and guide when that is apropos. Not every act of disobedience to God must be treated the same. Some acts are deliberate, others are not. Some Christians get themselves into trouble because of fear, others because of greed. Each circumstance requires a different response. And so it goes. Depending upon the nature of the problem—in whatever ways deficient faith leads to disobedience—the biblical counselor will work to bring about believing obedience. Continued and outspoken lack of faith ultimately may lead to church discipline. But a counselor will employ the spiritual weapon of church discipline only when necessary. There should be no rush to discipline.[1] It should be used only when a counselee continually refuses to "hear." It must be done incrementally, as Jesus described in Matthew 18:15 and following.[2] Putting a person out of the church, therefore, ought to be the last resort. Such action is based upon the fact that he refuses to exhibit faith in Christ's Word and, thereby, rejects His authority as it is vested in His church.

Many Christians, as I have noted, have lingering doubts about the wisdom of doing what the Scriptures say and are reluctant to obey or fear consequences if they do so.[3] It is to this matter that we shall direct our attention in the next chapter.

---

1 There is one exception to this rule: when a person is schismatic, according to Titus 3:10, he is to be dealt with quickly. The haste enjoined on the church in this passage stems presumably from the danger of such a person splitting the church by his schismatic behavior. Lingering over discipline, in such cases, is detrimental to the welfare of the congregation of which he is a part. Yet, even then, he is to be confronted at least once.

2 See my *Handbook of Church Discipline* for help.

3 Indeed, there is even lack of faith in church discipline. Many churches think they know better than Christ how to govern His church. This, on the part of church leaders, is not only sin, but a reprehensible failure to teach counselees and other members of the church. And it usually involves a lack of faith by these leaders.

6

Faith and Fear

More than once I have incidentally mentioned the problem of fear in relation to faith.[1] In those instances we noted how fear degrades faith. Perhaps the most frequent cause of lack of faith among Christians is fear. That is because the two are antithetical. It is faith that sustains Christians in the face of possible danger. That is precisely what Hebrews 11 exhibits over and over again. Whether freed from the dangers of possible persecution or sustained during it (even to the point of facing some terrible death), faith is what brought each of the Old Testament saints through victoriously. And that same sort of faith is what the writer of Hebrews calls upon you and your counselees to exercise as well.

But the problem is that, like the Hebrews, many Christians shrink back in fear when faced with possible danger or even difficulty. When that happens, it is important for the counselor to observe that the decision between fear and faith is under the counselee's control. The way his counselee responds to danger and difficulty is a matter of choice. He chooses to exercise faith or to become fearful. He will trust God or succumb to fear. The counselor must explicate the matter in full. Counselees think that

---

1 I am referring not to fear in general, but that fear which is occasioned by those situations in which the Bible says that one must not fear. Fear of falling over a cliff, for instance, makes one careful. Fear, in that sense, is perfectly acceptable. All emotions are God-given. They are not wrong in themselves. What makes them wrong is when they are aroused for unbiblical reasons or allowed to lead to unbiblical ends.

they have no control over fear. Of prime importance, then, is to show how it is possible to respond with faith rather than with fear.

What to Do

It is not difficult to set forth the choice. First, the counselee must be made to understand that he should not attempt to entertain both fear and faith simultaneously. Rather, he must recognize the antithesis between them and be called to make the choice. God will not permit him to settle for partial faith. Show him that failure to trust and obey God because of real or imagined[2] danger is sin. Recognition that even worry—let alone outright fearfulness— is sin is the first step in learning to trust God. Until a counselee understands this, he is not likely to have adequate motivation to do the hard things that God may require. Right there, of course, is the supreme concern: he must learn to overcome fear in order to honor and please God. He must be willing to put God's concerns before his own.[3] Fear in place of faith is a protest (however silent it may be) against God's providential working. It is an attack upon His judgment and goodness. Faith, on the other hand, expresses itself in the words of Romans 8:28: "God makes everything work together for the good of those who love Him." It is an acknowledgement of God's care and loving concern. Faith is a protest against temptation. When a counselee commits himself to doing what God requires of him regardless of the consequences, God will bless him and will strengthen the faith he already has.

---

2   Many supposed difficulties that counselees fear turn out to be imagined. In counseling, you often must point out that what a counselee fears is not likely to present the dangers he anticipates. "My parents will kill me if I tell them I was raped," is what one young girl said. The fact is, when she finally was persuaded to do so, they rushed in loving concern to embrace her!

3   Actually, God's interests, in the final analysis, are the best interests of a counselee though it is only by faith that he may be able to recognize this prior to the outcome.

An Important Advantage

One factor that a biblical counselor has in his favor is that he counsels Christians. That is, he counsels *believers*.[4] Though their faith may be small, all true Christians have faith. This is a given; there is no departure from it. If a person doesn't have faith, he is not a "believer." When a counselor is working with a believer, then, the counselor may appeal to the faith that he already possesses. In effect, with Paul he asks, "If God 'didn't spare His own Son, but delivered Him up for all of us, won't He also with Him freely give us everything?'" (Romans 8:32). That is to say, if God saved us from the very worst thing that could happen to us—eternal damnation—won't He rescue or sustain us in lesser matters? And if He went to the greatest length to do so by giving up His Son, won't He preserve us from lesser dangers as well? If there is faith to believe that God saved from hell, why isn't there faith to believe that He will care for us in all lesser matters? That is the crucial question.

Increasing Faith

But then, how does one increase his faith? Well, having recognized these facts that we have been reviewing, he must be reminded that "faith comes by hearing and hearing by the Word of Christ" (Romans 10:17). That is true of saving faith, but it is also true of subsequent faith. Why else did the writer of Hebrews go to such lengths to catalog the various experiences of the Old Testament saints if it was not his purpose to instill fearful readers with similar faith? Why did Paul say, "we pray very earnestly that we may see your face to supply whatever is lacking in your faith" if it wasn't possible to increase it (1 Thessalonians 3:10)? It was not his presence, per se, that would enlarge their faith, but his ability when present with them to speak the Word of God to them. It is God's Word, which today is found only in the Scriptures, that read,

---

4 People who have been given and possess faith.

understood, and believed causes faith to grow. As you open the Scriptures with counselees, explaining and applying them to their situations, you provide the very materials that help them increase their faith. Those counselors who fail to encourage faith by the use of God's Word can expect little growth. And, if it is important to challenge and strengthen counselees by means of Scripture ministered in counseling sessions, it is even more important to encourage their own, continued, independent Bible study as well.

There should be no question, then, that since the persons mentioned in Hebrews 11, all of whom in one way or another had to choose between faith or fear, were able to conquer through faith, your counselees also can do so. Never give up on them.[5]

---

5 For further help, see my pamphlet, *What Do You Do When Fear Overcomes You?*

7

Faith and Works

James and Paul

There is no need to discuss the supposed contradiction between James and Paul concerning faith and works. There is no such contradiction. Luther was wrong. The only distinction is in purpose and point of view. James comes to faith through works; Paul comes to works through faith. But though they come from the East and the West, they meet together as they end up in the same place. Both see an inseparable connection between true faith and acceptable good works.

The Counselor's Expectations

I am concerned about what *both* of these biblical writers affirm: that true faith always leads to works pleasing to God. And that fact is precisely what counselors must count upon and work with. They must assume that if the counselee is a genuine Christian, he not only can produce good works (through the power of the Spirit using the Word in conjunction with his renewed nature) but also that in time he can and will respond favorably to biblical counseling. With such hope, the biblical counselor undertakes counseling cheerfully, with large expectations. Biblical counselors counsel on the assumption that certain change is possible. They expect and work toward it with great anticipation. Therefore, the presence of faith, and the possibility that it may be enlarged by better understanding, agreement, and obedience to God's commands, emboldens them to call for significant change.

In a counseling session, the counselor may say, "Good! You say that you believe that God will help you get rid of lying if you ask Him and do as He says. Now, let's turn that statement of faith into actual practice by doing the following homework this week."

No Foolish Optimism

Of course, there is no foolish optimism in the preceding statement. Rather, counselors know that the change may come hard. They know that simply giving homework in no way implies that it will be done. They counsel with no false notions about the readiness of counselees to do all that they should. James surely didn't, or he would not have written to the church as he did. They recognize that at times there will be resistance, retrogression, and even downright disobedience. But since they know that all of the necessary ingredients for change are present, they counsel with confidence. That is because they place their confidence in the unfailing Word of God. They work and look for change.

It is only after continued counselee failure, a careful self-analysis of the counsel given, and all other possible failure factors, that counselors begin to question the genuineness of the counselee's faith. Until that occurs, they continue to work in faith for the faithful work that *God* will do in His counselee.

Faith and Works Central

The concept of faith leading to works lies at the very heart of the counseling process. It is because of the integral nature of the two that biblical counselors counsel as they do. Many other counselors think that counseling is a matter of what goes on in the counseling session. It is here that any change that may take place will occur: the counselor becomes the magician who "does it" for the counselee, and the counseling session is the magic hour in which he does it. In contrast, the biblical counselor sees the counseling session as that time in which faith is encouraged, strengthened, and firmly fixed upon the Word of God as well as the God of the Word. Faith is, therefore, utterly essential. It is in these sessions that God's will is set forth from the Scriptures, objections and misunderstandings are dealt with, and application to the counselee's situation and commitments to do homework are made. These commitments for the week to come set forth in terms of "homework" (that is, work that grows out of the expressions of understanding and agreement made during sessions) are intended to lead to works pleasing to God. During the week, the counselee further expresses his faith in works. So, it is clear that the very structure of the counseling process is based upon the faith/works dynamic.

Counseling Structured Upon the Faith/Works Dynamic

The faith that is forthcoming during counseling sessions must be faith that is anchored in truth that is clearly understood. True faith, as we saw, always flows from understanding of God's truth. In the sessions, the second element—agreement—also occurs. Biblical counselors should not knowingly send someone out to do what he does not understand or does not agree he ought to do. The third element of trust (or dependence) is manifested in doing the homework. It is here that faith comes into its fullness as understanding and agreement lead to actually doing those works that were previously understood and agreed upon. The counselee must go forth to obey God implicitly, in dependence upon what He promises in His Word.

Things Aren't Always Easy

Now, of course, I am expressing the ideal. There are, as I said previously, many difficult times along the way toward arriving at biblical change. These must be dealt with as I have described in many other books, and cannot be explicated here. But what I wish to affirm is that whatever is done to help counselees must always be done within the faith/works framework. There is no reason ever to depart from it. Counselees who declare that they understand and agree with God's Word must always be called upon to express that understanding and agreement by doing the works that are implied in both.

This means that at some point, when there is a problem that impedes counseling, a principal way to go about discovering the reason for it is to look into each of the aspects of faith. Is there a problem of understanding? Did you not make the biblical injunction clear? Did the counselee listen selectively? Has he been taught a false understanding of some biblical doctrine? You can, of course, go on asking other appropriate questions.

If there is no problem with understanding what God desires of him, then investigate the counselee's assent. Does he agree that he should do as the Bible says? If not, then what stands in the way? Is it fear? Is it previous failure? Is it because he is devoted to some sin that he doesn't want to part with? Is it because he admires someone else and does not wish to hurt him? Or disagree with him? And so on.

Or if there is understanding and agreement, you should then pursue the matter of his commitment to doing what God wants. If he understands and agrees that he should go and confess his sins to another, for example, then what is it that is keeping him from doing so? Embarrassment? Fear of consequences? Something else? Investigate the problem thoroughly. What stands between him and dependence upon God's promises?

In one way or another, then, you can see the need to look into the matter of a counselee's faith. Obviously, as I said earlier, you cannot know his heart, but you can investigate each aspect of faith with him to help him see what is wrong. If you do so properly, together you will be able to discover what is lacking in his faith.

Works Involved in Faith

That faith is all-pervasive in the biblical counseling process ought to be evident. Anything that a counselor or counselee does must be done in faith or it isn't a good work. And when a counselee does deeds pleasing to God, what he does is so much a part of faith that the two cannot be separated. This should be clear from the fact that dependence (the culminating aspect of faith) is inseparably merged with the deed itself. Jesus Himself made this point:

> Then they said to Him, "What should we do to accomplish God's works?" Jesus answered them with these words: "This is God's work—that you believe in Him Whom He has sent."
>
> (John 6:28, 29)

Clearly, Jesus did not confuse faith and works. But it seems certain that he did not see so great a disjunction between them as some do. For Him, to believe was to trust. It was a "work," He said. There was so close a connection between faith and works that neither could not exist without the other. Surely, that is why James so plainly affirms that true faith always results in works. That is why he was so clear about the fact that without works, faith is dead. Faith and works are separable, so that one can do works that are not born of faith as, unfortunately, many do, but he calls them "dead works." He says that such works are like the dead body from which the spirit has departed. Except in an academic, analytical manner, the spirit and the body cannot be separated without killing the person. If the spirit leaves the body, it is no longer a living body.

Similarly, when faith is removed from works, they are no longer God-pleasing works—they are as dead as that lifeless body.[1]

Call Your Counselees To Do Works of *Faith*

Since these things are true, you can see can't you, that it is utterly important to be sure to call upon a counselee to do what God requires of him—*in faith*. To attempt to please God with dead works is the height of folly. It is contrary to God's order. It deceives the counselee into thinking that he can please God in his own wisdom and strength. And it misrepresents God.

So when you send him out to do homework, make a point of the need to do it in faith. Tell him, "You must give up fornication. Leave that woman with whom you have been living. As you do so, you must believe that you will be pleasing God, that as you ask He will help you, and that as you obey His Word He will bless you." It is not enough merely to say, "Joe, you know that fornication is wrong. It's harmful to everyone involved. So, this week, make a clean break with that woman." The second admonition is wrong in two ways: 1) The reason given—that it is harmful—is on a horizontal level. Of course it is, but there is no vertical dimension in the statement. Joe is not exhorted to change for God's sake; 2) Joe is sent to do what he is told to do in his own strength. There is no promise that God will be with him as, indeed, He may not.[2] In both of these failings, the central issue is whether or not God is in the counselee's picture.

Of course, no one can really remove God from the picture; His providential working always takes place. But a counselor must make that fact evident to his counselee. He must place before him an accurate picture. Fundamentally, he must call upon him to obey

---

1   Cf. James 2:14, 17, 22, 26.
2   But God is often more gracious to us than we would be to ourselves, were we to see things rightly!

God in faith. All purely horizontal works are "dead works" because they are not done in faith. That is the core of the matter.

8

How About the Counselor?

Whether or not the counselor has faith is important, but it does not *necessarily* determine the outcome of the counseling case.[1] It is possible for a counselee to have stronger faith than his counselor does. The situation ought not to exist, and probably does only in exceptional instances, but that possibility should not be ignored. What might lead to such an eventuality? There are several possibilities.

Some Counselors Lack Faith
to Do God's Works

First, a counselor who in his own life has been frequently unsuccessful in handling a problem that is similar to that of the counselee may have little hope or faith in what he may say to his counselee. He may mouth what he disbelieves. This deplorable eventuality ought not to occur, as I said. While not perfect, a counselor ought to be successfully working at growth in all aspects of his life. That is what James meant when he spoke of becoming *teleios* (James explained the term when he wrote of being "complete and entire, lacking in nothing"; 1:4). The word "complete" is *teleios*.[2] If a counselor is failing to work on his own problems *in all*

---

1 Here I am referring to the faith of a genuine, biblical counselor, not a liberal or pretender.
2 For more about this, see my study of the book of James called *A Thirst for Wholeness*.

areas of life, the process of sanctification in his life is not "complete." He may change this condition, according to James, if he will ask of God (James 1:5) and receive wisdom from the Word to become a successful, Godly counselor.

A counselor also may lack the faith to expect change in a counselee because he may have bought into some false idea. There are many such ideas abroad that may weaken faith. If, for instance, he has come to believe that homosexuality is genetic, he is not likely to put much stock in helping a homosexual change, even if the latter wants to do so.[3] Or he may accept Alcoholics Anonymous' (AA) teaching that says a drunkard can never fully put his problem with drink behind him once for all. He must go on reminding himself every day that he is a drunkard.[4]

Prejudice Can Get in the Way

Prejudicial attitudes may get in the counselor's way if he fails to overcome them. For instance, he may think, "Oh well, some people are just like that. I doubt that there will be any change at all." Or, he may believe a counselee is too old to change very much: "You can't teach an old dog new tricks." He may despair of persons from different cultures and races: "That problem seems to be endemic to those sorts of people." He may say, "He comes from a long line of liars. How can we expect anything else from him?" In all of these instances, the counselor may expect very little from the counselee. The biblical teaching about culturally conditioned behavior, whether it was learned in the home or elsewhere, is that it may be replaced. Take home patterns, for instance. Listen to a close translation of 1 Peter 1:17–19:

---

3 Cf. Romans 1:24–32, where God says that homosexuality as well as other sins are deliberate.

4 Cf. 1 Corinthians 6:9–11, in which we see that some in Corinth *did* put this behind them.

If you call Him Father Who impartially judges each one by his deeds, then be deeply concerned about how you behave during your residence as aliens, knowing that you weren't set free from the useless behavior patterns that were passed down from your forefathers by the payment of a corruptible ransom like silver or gold, but with Christ's valuable blood.

In such cases the counselor himself must change his unbelief if he seriously wants to help others. Indeed, because of his disbelief he may settle for too little change, thinking that this is all that is possible. His goals are too low if they are not God's goals. In such cases, his failure to help a counselee is the outcome of a self-fulfilling prophecy! And, when that happens, he becomes more entrenched in his disbelief, thinking, "I knew it!"

Counselors Must Change

If and when a counselor recognizes his problem, what must he do? First, he should cease from counseling until his doubts are replaced by faith. Others don't need to be adversely influenced by his doubt.[5] He must then repent of his unbelief to God and to the counselee. And when he resumes counseling, this time he should do so with the faith that he should have had in the beginning.

Usually, the counselor loses no authority in changing. His counselee may even learn from his honesty. Making an about face only emphasizes the fact to the counselee that change is possible. When that happens, counseling may take on new life. Admission

---

5   Of course, if he is in the middle of a series of counseling sessions, he might 1) call in another counselor to sit in or, if that is impossible; 2) he may simply confess to the counselee that he has been counseling with doubt and that he plans to immediately change his perspective on what they are doing. Then, in newly found faith, he may move ahead. It is easier to make an about face when one admits some failure to a counselee.

of doubt on the part of the counselor may even lead to a counseling breakthrough.[6] And his outright admission of previous failure, at the very least, will clarify where counseling has gone wrong.[7]

Every counselor from time to time ought to examine his beliefs, disbeliefs, doubts, and prejudices. Self-examination, however, must never become morbid or debilitating. Having recognized his problem, repented, and turned about face, he must move ahead, counseling properly. Disbelief in one's self is healthy only when it leads to greater faith in God. And when it leads to biblical change, it becomes healthy and faithstrengthening.

So, counselor, is it time to examine yourself?

---

6 See my book, *Critical Stages in Biblical Counseling,* for information on the breakthrough stage.

7 If a counselor simply shifts course, without such an admission, the shift may confuse the counselee.

9

Can You Trust Your Counselee?

This is a hard one. You know that every counselee, like yourself, is a sinner. You know that you are not always trustworthy; you know that he isn't either. So, how can you trust him? Should you? Is it even right to trust in any man? Doesn't Jeremiah warn us about this (17:5)? Well, like many other things, the answer is "yes and no." As we progress, you will see what I mean by that.

The problem has many dimensions. Of course no one should trust in man rather than in the Lord; indeed, that is the real point of Jeremiah 17:5. No one should trust in man implicitly. No one should trust in man without evaluating what he does or says according to the standard of the Scriptures. If that's so, then how does one trust a counselee?

You Counsel Believers

We can trust a believer—to a large extent—since he is a believer. God does a work in the heart of every one whom He saves to enable him to think His thoughts after Him and to do His works as well. In other words, there is much more reason to trust a believer than an unbeliever. His faith makes all the difference.

He is imperfect and still retains the remnants of sin that he carried over from his former, unsaved life. Yet, because of the work of God in his soul, at the very least there is an element of integrity in him. With Paul, the counselor can say that he is "confident of this, that He Who began a good work among you will keep on perfecting it until the Day of Jesus Christ" (Philippians 1:6). The translation is in question as to whether the preposition ought to be translated "in" or "among." Both are possible, but the latter seems preferable. Nevertheless, the fact that is conveyed is true of a body of Christians viewed as a whole and of the individual Christians who make up that body. So, what Paul said to the church at Philippi, he also said to each member. Because of God's "good work," it is possible to think of a counselee as trustworthy to the extent that He is at work in him to make him so.

Loving Counsel

That is the reason why Paul could exhort his readers that love "believes all things" (1 Corinthians 13:7). To believe the word of a fellow Christian is to show love toward him. Freud thought that all motivation stemmed from the unconscious, and that the conscious word of a client had to be challenged under all circumstances since it was mere rationalization. The truth could be obtained only by bringing it to consciousness through psychoanalysis. He did not believe his clients, and he certainly did not love them.

A true Christian counselor is not Freudian. A biblical counselor believes that his counselees mostly want to tell the truth. He knows that it is often slanted by self-interest, that it may be inaccurate and that a counselee even may be lying. Nevertheless, the Christian counselor has faith in what God says about showing love to a counselee by believing him as far as possible. He certainly doesn't think that he must dredge the truth from his unconscious! He doesn't think that it is necessary to challenge everything that he says as rationalization. So he believes the counselee unless the facts prove otherwise.

How can a believer keep from being a "patsy?" How can he keep from transgressing Proverbs 14:15 where we are told that it is foolishness to believe every word? Well, that's the point. He believes what is possible to believe—not every word. He knows that the words of no counselees are infallible—not even those of Christians. But he does have a predisposition to believe what he can, which is a far different thing than doubting everything said as mere rationalization of unconscious motivation.

Your Appeal

Because he believes that God has done a good work in his counselee, he appeals to this. He asks God to help the counselee to tell the truth as fully and accurately as possible. Indeed, he recognizes that sometimes as the counselee discloses matters that are difficult for him to say, that very act itself may constitute a spurt of growth in which God is perfecting His work in the counselee. With this prayerful, loving disposition, the Christian counselor most frequently obtains much truth by simply asking his counselee to explain what is burdening him.

But what if he lies? Again I ask, how does the counselor keep from being a "patsy?" How does he avoid being led down the garden path? Well, he does so by following biblical instructions. For instance, in Proverbs 18:15, we are told that one person who tells his story seems correct until another comes and examines him. The counselor, therefore, wants to get data from all concerned parties, so far as that is possible. If he can't, he refuses to accept negative information about another who isn't present because it is gossip. He requires two or three witnesses to all such material (2 Corinthians 13:1). The fact that a counselee is unable to do assigned homework (following the idea that faith must lead to works), often discloses lying. Homework should be based on prior data submitted by a counselee. So if the data are false he may not be able to accomplish what the homework requires. Probing failure to do homework may show that previous data were untrue.

So, you see, the Christian counselor has a predisposition to believe his counselees. And he will do so unless there are biblical reasons not to.

10

Where Faith Comes From

While it is the Christian who exercises faith, he himself is not the one who generates or even increases it. Faith is "the gift of God" (Ephesians 2:8). No one who is "dead in trespasses and sins" (v. 1) is able to exercise biblical faith without divine assistance. And when God gives faith to enable someone to believe, He gives it in different measures: "I tell every one of you: 'Don't think more highly of yourself than you ought to, but think soberly according to the measure of faith that God distributed to each of you' " (Romans 12:3).

Now, That Raises an Important Issue

You may ask, "But, if God is the source of faith, surely He should not hold those who lack faith guilty, should He? And further, if some have little faith while others have more, since *He* determined the measure of faith given to each, why would Jesus complain about people having but little faith? Indeed, if God determines the amount of faith He will distribute to each Christian, what use is it for a counselor to exhort or try to help his counselees to increase their faith?" These are critically important questions. They should not be lightly bypassed since many are confused about them. Wrongly answered, they can lead to bitter discouragement or utter failure in counseling.

God certainly does hold people responsible for faith or the lack thereof. Speaking of saving faith in Christ, we read, "Whoever … doesn't believe in Him is already judged because he hasn't believed in the name of God's unique Son" (John 3:18). And Jesus reproved Peter for having too little faith, even calling him by the nickname "Little-Faith," as we have seen. Now, because we know from these and many other passages that God does hold unbelievers responsible for the lack of saving faith, and Christians responsible for faith that brings about their sanctification, we can readily see the problem. Therefore, we must reconcile the seeming contradiction.

There is No Contradiction

We know that there is no contradiction. God never contradicts Himself or frustrates His own work. There must be perfect harmony in all of this. How can the matter be cleared up? By recognizing that God enables us to do what we ourselves cannot do. What does that mean? Prior to regeneration (the giving of spiritual life) we were unable to do anything that pleased God. "Those who are in the flesh cannot please God" (Romans 8:8). To be "in the flesh" is to be unsaved, spiritually dead in sin. But God did what we were unable to do: "Even when we were dead in trespasses, [God] made us alive ... with Christ" (Ephesians 2:5). Because we received spiritual life we were able to believe. Our eyes were opened[1] to the truth of the gospel, and we trusted Christ as Savior. We believed because the Spirit made it possible to do so, and gave us the desire to believe in Christ. But *we* believed. So, there was God's part and man's part; neither of which is opposed or contrary to the other in any way. Actually, they work together in perfect harmony.

You may then reply, "OK. I can see that. But what of the distribution (or measure) of faith?" Again, it is important to remember that the human and the divine work together toward the same ends. "How is that?" Well, God requires faith of us so that

---

1 Before we had eyes but could not see (1 Corinthians 2:9). As Paul says in this chapter, the Spirit alone can enable one to understand the things He has revealed. It is through His Spirit, then, that we are given life to believe. This is how faith is "given."

we will grow as Christians. But remember, growth is the fruit of the Spirit (Galatians 5). As He was the One to give us life to believe, so too He is the One who enables us to grow. Peter exhorts his readers to "grow by the grace [help] and the knowledge of our Lord and Savior Jesus Christ" (2 Peter 3:18). Growing is not something we can do without His gracious enabling. Paul put it this way: "It is God Who is producing in you both the willingness and the ability to do the things that please Him" (Philippians 2:13).[2] Once more, God gives the desire and the capability to do His will, and then we do it.

"But ... but ... but ..."

Hold on a minute. I think I know what you are going to say. You still don't see that God is the One by Whom all that is worthwhile is achieved and how He can rightly hold us responsible when we fail to live up to the biblical standard. The answer is simple—but profound. He has planned both the end *and the means*. It is not as though God purposed certain events (e.g., our faith or lack of it) but somehow left us to find the ways to bring them about. It is not that someone's faith would fail regardless of what he wished. No. He also purposed the means by which all events would come to pass. And the means was—don't miss this— through the responsible actions of responsible human beings. That is to say, human agency is at work in the process of bringing about God's purposes. *We* believe; God does not believe *for* us. But if we fail to exercise faith when we should, it is we who fail, not the Spirit of God in us. We are responsible for our doubts because God holds us responsible to have faith. Now, I understand that this is difficult but I cannot go further into the matter here. For detailed biblical argumentation about this and kindred matters, see my book, *The*

---

2   F. F. Bruce put it well: "The new covenant was secured by the indwelling Spirit of God, not only enlightening his people with the knowledge of his will, but supplying the desire and the power to do it." *Searching Together*, Taylor Falls. Winter: 2002, Vol. 30:4, p. 6.

Grand Demonstration, a Biblical Study of the So-called Problem of Evil.

God's Purpose

In order to comprehend what I have been talking about, it is essential to get a firm grip on both the purpose and the providence of God. God plans His work then He works His plan. The eternal purpose of God is to bring about His glory by ordering the universe and all that is within it to do so. This purpose does not fail. God cannot be frustrated. Even when we do those things that displease Him, our sin redounds to His glory because this makes it possible for both His mercy and His grace to be exhibited in it. As He deals with us, the various sides of His nature are revealed. When there are others who do not believe and are not saved, He is not frustrated because His divine justice and wrath are manifested as He deals with them.

God's Providence

I must also say this: that God works providentially means that He did not merely create the world and then walk away from it. He is not interested only in ends, but also in means. And, He superintends the courses of men and events, and all factors that pertain to them. He is present at work in His world. He is the ever-present God! Indeed, as Paul indicated in his speech at Athens, our life and every breath are sustained by Him (Acts 17:25).

Counseling

But what has all of this to do with counseling? These facts should encourage and cause joy for those who counsel. If God's will is going to prevail, we know that change in our counselees doesn't depend ultimately upon what we do or our counselees do. That is to say, our faith and theirs grow by God's grace, not by our prowess. It also means that we recognize that responsibility is ours—not ultimately, but proximately—because as agents who achieve (or fail to achieve) God's will we are responsible for our decisions. We are not working alone. God is there, giving us (and our counselees) both the willingness and the ability to do those things that please Him. We call upon God to help us and urge our counselees to do the same. We can do this because we know that God gives grace to the humble (as we saw in an earlier chapter, James 4:6). He is actually at work in us and in our counselees. Faith, and its increase, are both possible. We are not like those who believe that if God were to answer prayers by changing our desires and the determinations, He would be violating our "free will." No, we are God's creatures, entirely subject to His every will for us.

Faith, then, is a divinely given attribute. Let us grow in it. Let us thank God for it. And, recognizing our dependence upon Him for faith, let us praise Him for the mercy He has shown to us and our counselees. Gratitude is born out of faith.

11

Faith and Promise

True biblical faith focuses upon the promise, not upon its fulfillment. This is a difficult, but important, lesson for counselees (counselors, for that matter) to learn. You will be wise to dwell on this point in counseling, coming back to it as you deem necessary. We all want to see the outcome of our faith here and now. But often that isn't how God does things. He may wait until later, even until eternity, to fulfill His promises. That is what Hebrews 11:13 tells us: "these all died in faith without receiving the things that were promised." Does that mean God fails to keep His Word? No, he had a better fulfillment of His promises than an earthly one would have been. The physical aspects of the promises were but a type of the spiritual reality.

Once More, Consider Those Saints
in Hebrews 11

Some promises are fulfilled in the present time, while others are not. The saints in Hebrews 11 who only saw the things promised from far off, nevertheless, were given the faith that God promised them to endure hardships, deprivation, and horrible deaths when they most needed it. In this chapter we see that some promises were fulfilled in this life; others only after death. And the outcomes of faith greatly differed. While the faith of all was equal, the outcomes of their faith were not: some died for their faith; others achieved great victories in this life. That is important for counselees to see. In this, God has His eternal purposes which, as we saw in the previous chapter, He brings to pass in time.

Faith means believing God's promises by fully understanding, agreeing, and depending on them. "By faith" the Christian must look forward to what God will do when, where, and how He pleases. Many never entered into the promises in this life, but did "see them from a distance, and welcomed them" (Hebrews 11:13). They looked beyond temporal fulfillment to that better city whose Builder and Maker is God. They welcomed the future promises because they believed that these were a better fulfillment than any temporal one could ever be.

Many counselees want change now. The prayer, "Lord, please give me patience—and do so now" says it all. God often works patience in His children by passing them through trials: "the testing of your faith works endurance" (James 1:3). In the midst of trial, your counselee will discover how solid his faith may be. The fires of testing, like those of a furnace used to test and purify precious metals, are seldom pleasant but always necessary (cf. 1 Peter 1:6, 7). As Hebrews 11 shows, and James 1:1–2 tells us, these trials may be of various sorts.

What If It Seems There Can Be No Fulfillment?

Now, the interesting thing is that, at times, the promises of God may even seem impossible of fulfillment. The proposed sacrifice of Isaac by Abraham is a case in point. Isaac was the son through whose posterity all of the covenant promises of God were to be fulfilled. But when God said "Sacrifice him," Abraham prepared to do so. He was trusting that, in one way or another, God would keep His promises. Indeed, his faith was so strongly focused upon the faithfulness of God that he figured out a way in which He might fulfill them in spite of the sacrifice: He reasoned that God might raise Isaac from the dead (v. 19). His conjecture was wrong, but his unwavering faith in God's promise was right! That is often the way that it is: God promises, but we cannot see how He can bring it to pass. In such instances, counselees must be encouraged to trust God's Word. Help them to focus on His promises rather than on their fulfillment. Trust the promises and leave the fulfillment to Him!

A Protest and an Explanation

When counselees protest, "But God promised …," you must explain that He did not necessarily promise that what would happen would do so when and how they wanted it to. In 1 Corinthians 10:13, Paul says that God "will provide together with the trial the way out so that you may be able to endure it." How? When? Some will escape by being rescued from a problem, others by death. That is the sort of difference counselees must be taught. There is no earthly Pollyanna solution to every difficulty. A husband may determine to divorce his wife (and do so) even though she prayed for a different solution to the problems in her marriage. By faith, she should accept the "way out" that God has prepared rather than her own.

The importance of this matter should be obvious. Think through the implications of the biblical principles involved in this matter. You will be dealing with them frequently. To summarize: faith centers upon God's promises, not upon their fulfillment.

12

Is Faith a Risk?

Kierkegaard spoke of the "leap of faith." By that he meant faith is a leap in the dark. Pascal settled for a wager that there is a God—as the best bet. All such thinking stems from the idea of risk. Is exercising faith taking a risk? Certainly not!

You may wonder, "But what of those saints in Hebrews 11 that you keep on referring to? Surely they risked their fortunes, their families, their wellbeing, and even their lives. And what about Epaphroditus who Paul explicitly said risked his life (Philippians 2:25–30)?"

I insist that it is true to say that faith is not risk. Indeed, faith is solidly grounded assurance that what God says is true. Where is the risk in that? If one trusts himself to the guidance, care, and keeping of God while obeying His Word, how can there be any risk at all? God keeps His promises, as we have seen. There is no risk of failure. Since that is true, where is the risk?

Of course, from another point of view, one does take risks when he trusts God's Word. Like Epaphroditus, who became sick and risked his life in order to serve Paul in prison, from time to time counselees must take such risks as those. But notice the difference: One may risk danger or even death while fully trusting in God. To live and act in faith may lead him into either, but there is no risk regarding the outcome. He will be victorious like the saints to whom the promises in Jesus' letters to the seven churches were given, the believer today can be assured of a victorious outcome. Risk has solely to do with men; there is no risk with God.

But when a believer risks persecution by obeying God, ultimately even that is not a risk at all. It is part of the providential working out of God's plan to bring all things together for His glory and the believer's good (Romans 8:28). Trusting and obeying God is never risky when one takes the long view. That is what the saints in Hebrews 11 knew. Indeed, it is even said of Moses that he chose mistreatment with God's people rather than retain his right to the riches of Egypt *"because he was looking ahead to the reward"* (v. 26, emphasis mine). He chose the eternal Christ over temporal Egypt because he *saw* the One Who is unseen (v. 27). By faith, a believing counselee must see beyond present advantages to the time when he will receive the reward which is incorruptible and cannot fade or be taken away. The one with faith knows that there is no eternal risk, though at present he may risk persecution.

But even apart from the eternal fulfillment of the better reward, in faith one should understand that *in the present time* there is no risk, as the world understands risk. Should trials come his way, as we have seen, they are for his benefit. Should a counselee encounter opposition and derision from others when he acts in faith, he knows that the Lord smiles upon him. The pleasure that comes from pleasing Him trumps everything else. The only real risk that he runs is failure to love and obey God through lack of faith. Now, that is truly risky!

So the very idea of faith means that the one who believes has transcended the possibility of genuine risk. His faith triumphs over fear, over doubt, over everything else. Listen to Paul in Romans 8:

> Who can separate us from Christ's love? Can affliction, or distress, or persecution, or famine, or nakedness, or danger or sword?... No! In all of these things we are more

than conquerors through the One Who loved us (vv. 35, 37; see also vv. 38, 39).

If Paul is right, and we know that he is, where is the risk? Why is a wager necessary? Or a leap of faith? What on earth is that leap but whistling in the dark? And why would it be necessary for one who knows the living Christ? Even here in this life there is no real risk. By taking "risks" (humanly speaking), a counselee experiences more of the love of Jesus Christ. And, in whatever comes his way, you can assure your counselee who acts in faith that he will only know the love of Christ manifested somehow in it.

So is there a risk? You can answer that for yourself. But, unless you help your counselee to reach the same answer, he is likely not to see it. Spend time with fearful counselees discussing the matter of risk-taking from a biblical perspective. Christianity is not a gamble!

13

The Enabling Power of Faith

In a number of places in the Scriptures, we are told that faith enables the Christian to engage successfully in activities that God expects of him. Faith is said to enable him to walk, to stand, to fight, to overcome, to endure. Here we shall look at a few examples.

Perseverance

Perseverance comes through faith. In 2 Corinthians 1:24, Paul speaks of members of the church at Corinth "standing firm by faith." This is one of the most important effects of faith. In the midst of trial and persecution (as we have seen by our examination of Hebrews 11), it was faith that enabled the Old Testament worthies to endure. In a day in which there is much to endure in many parts of a world in turmoil, it is good to know that this is how God preserves His own. He keeps them true to Him by faith. In discussing the matter of perseverance, Peter wrote that believers are "guarded by God's power through faith for a salvation that is ready to be revealed in the last time" (1 Peter 1:5). Faith is the means by which the believer is kept from apostasy.

God's Power Released in Faith

Now, we should understand that it is "God power" that is at work producing and maintaining faith in the believer. Notice the construction of the verses in 1 Peter 1:3–5. God regenerates us, lays up our inheritance and keeps it so that nothing can harm it, and guards us as heirs by His power "through faith." It is His power that enables us to continue to the end (the fullness of our salvation yet to be revealed). Faith is the instrument by which God does this work. It is not faith in and of itself, then, that guards and preserves us, rather it is God's power. But while He powerfully works in us, it is to produce and maintain our faith by which we persevere. There is no vague "keep the faith" idea here. It is God-given faith. Because that faith is from God, we can take heart that true believers will persevere. This is the truth that some who doubt their salvation need to hear, and it is also one that all counselees who are discouraged and defeated need to rest upon. The counselor, moreover, ought to take heart in this fact.

Walking by Faith

In addition to perseverance by faith, the Christian's entire "walk" is to be by faith. Paul wrote, "We walk by faith, not by sight" (2 Corinthians 5:7). By faith, the Christian is enabled to reach out beyond temporal circumstances to the eternal power and plan of God. Faith resides in God Who is invisible. So trusting in Him, we walk by faith. What is the Christian's walk? As I have shown elsewhere, the word "walk" (a Hebrew expression for the habitual or regular conduct of one's affairs) refers to one's lifestyle. This walk is to be a righteous walk, first with God, then with other believers and in relation to the world. In Ephesians 5 and 6, Paul speaks frequently about this walk giving direction to the believer. Psalm 1 sets the theme for many other Psalms as it compares and contrasts the walks of the righteous and the unrighteous.

A Different Drumbeat

Now, it is matters having to do with the Christian's daily lifestyle that counselors are concerned about. They want to help their counselees to conform more closely to the "walk" of Jesus Christ. Large among those things that they will stress is the necessity to walk *by faith*. A counselee must recognize that God requires him to walk according to a different drum beat—one that sounds forth from heaven. When he does, he will be so out of step with the world that he breaks lines with those he once marched with. But he will never do so if he adheres to the cadence of those around him. To change direction, to walk alone, to march against the crowd is an essential part of counseling advice to one who is in lockstep with the world. How will that change? When the drumbeat of heaven beats more loudly in his ears than that of the world around him. To part company with friends and even relatives requires faith. But, as we have seen, it is God who provides and maintains this faith. Call upon your counselee who is having difficulty separating from sinful ways and those around him to listen by faith to the heavenly marching band as they tread their way through Hebrews 11 and elsewhere!. This new cadence of life is encouraged by surrounding one's self with the promises of God. Tell him so.

Faith for the Fight

In 1 Timothy 6:12, Paul calls on Timothy to "fight the gallant fight of faith." The Christian life is a walk—often straight into the face of the enemy. It is not a parade down main street, but a march into the world's territory. There are battles to be fought, wounds to be healed, and comrades to be rescued. How will battles be fought? Paul says, through faith. What does faith do to strengthen and enable the believer to fight gallantly? It enables him to see the outcome even before the battle. He knows that God will win, and that he is on the winning side. While not lessening its ferocity, that should make the battle bearable. One can fight gallantly when he recognizes that he is on the right side. It is by faith that he knows all of these things—and more. As you counsel a defeated counselee who is about to give up the battle, remind him of the One for Whom he fights, of the power and strength that He provides, and of the outcome of the battle. Once he becomes enthusiastic about these things, he will sally forth again to the front lines. But these matters are all comprehended by faith. They are not evident to those without faith which alone enables a Christian to see even in the darkest night. That night vision capability, which the enemy doesn't have, is uppermost in the battle.

No Defeat is Allowed

To add to this, one ought to mention 1 John 5:4: "Whoever has been born of God defeats the world. And this is what defeats the world: our faith." You will find this verse of great help in counseling defeated Christians. It explains why they are experiencing defeat—perhaps over and over again. It is time for them to repent and believe the promises of God. Repentance, remember, involves changing both one's mind and one's walk.[1] At first, defeated Christians may not think that repentance is the proper response to defeat. Instead, they may cry for sympathy. But you can explain from I John that the way that God sees it is that there is no room in the Christian's walk for defeat. In 2 Corinthians 10:3–6, Paul explains that our weapons are more powerful through God than those of our opponents. There is, therefore, no excuse for defeat. Faith is the answer to defeat because it overcomes (defeats) the world. Faith is believing God's promises, as we have seen. If this is true, then we must accept the promises in 2 Corinthians 10 and 1 John 5:4 and do battle. Defeat comes from lack of faith. In conclusion, let me mention several verses that will prove useful. We read in Revelation 2:7: "To the one who has defeated the enemy, I shall give the right to eat of the tree of life that is in God's paradise." In Revelation 2:10 Christ says, "Be faithful to death and I shall give the winner's wreath of life to you." In Revelation 2:17, Jesus promises to "give

---

1 The New Testament word *metanoia* means "rethinking; changing the mind." The Old Testament term *shuv* means "turning around." Together, they show that repentance is a change of mind leading to a change of direction. Since our thoughts are not God's thoughts and our ways are not His ways (Isaiah 55:8), repentance brings us in line with both.

some of the hidden manna and ... a white stone with a fresh new name written on it." The promise in Revelation 2:26 reads, "To the one who defeats the enemy and keeps doing the deeds I command ... authority over the nations." In Revelation 3:4–5, the promise is "white clothing" in which to "walk" with Christ. In Revelation 3:12, He promises that "whoever defeats the enemy I shall make a pillar in My God's temple ... and I shall write on him the Name of My God, and the Name of the new Jerusalem ... and My fresh new Name." And finally, in Revelation 3:21, Jesus says, "To the one who defeats the enemy I shall grant the right to sit with Me on My throne, just as I defeated him and sat down with My Father on His throne."

With such promises, who should fail? These verses remind us that the defeat of our enemies promised by faith brings with it innumerable eternal blessings. Discouraged, defeated Christians need to hear God's promises.

14

When Faith Isn't Easy

When there is danger, difficulty, or discouragement involved in doing God's will, faith may falter. When you are persecuted, ostracized or scorned, it is difficult to remain strong in faith. But it isn't about any of those matters that I am concerned in this chapter. Here, the problem of wanting one's way when it is contrary to Scripture is my interest.

A Case in Point

Margaret wants to marry Bill. She knows that it isn't biblical to do so since the Scripture forbids marrying an unbeliever (according to 1 Corinthians 7:39 she is to marry "only in the Lord"). Yet her faith is weak because her desire is strong. After all, she has seldom dated, she is growing older, and this seems to be her last chance to marry. "Surely, the Lord doesn't want me to abandon this opportunity. Bill is so nice, and I probably could lead him to the Lord after marriage," she reasons. Her desire and her rationalizations lead her to conclude that in her case there ought to be an exception to Paul's rule. Counselors frequently face the problem of a counselee's desire weakening and temporarily overcoming faith. What can a counselor say to those who are convinced their way is right in spite of what the Bible teaches? How does he respond to those who claim to know more than God?

There are Resources to Help

Peter addresses the matter in his first epistle, He writes, "As children who are under obedience, don't shape your lives by the desires that you used to follow in your ignorance" (1 Peter 1:14). In that sentence there are several points that a counselor may make when dealing with the counselee whose desire is about to trump his faith. Notice, first of all, that Peter appeals to the fact that we are not to follow our desire as we did before we were saved. Next, consider the motivation for biblical obedience: it is by His grace that you have become a child of God (v. 13)! And as children, you are to obey your heavenly Father. Moreover, it is your responsibility to "shape your lives" in accordance with God's commands, since you are "under obedience" to Him. And last, since you have been enlightened by the Spirit of God, you can no longer excuse your disobedience as ignorance of His will. A counselor may ring the changes on these facts.

But that isn't all. In the next verse, Peter continues his emphasis: "Instead, as the One Who called you is holy, you yourselves must become holy in all your behavior." Your counselees are to be like their Father. To be holy as He is holy is the goal for their lives. The word "holy" means to be "set apart." When God sets apart a person as His child, he expects him to manifest the family traits. He becomes part of a new family. He says, "Like Father, like son." When a son (or daughter) fails to live according to the family's rules, which are not like the evil one's rules, he confuses the issue for those who know him. And of greater moment—he brings disgrace upon his Father. So in these verses, you find several strong reasons for obedience.

This latter fact is spelled out in verse 17: "If you call Him Father Who impartially judges each one by his deeds, then be deeply concerned about how you behave during your residence as aliens." The believer's home is with the Father—in the heavenly

Jerusalem. He is but a resident alien here. He is a member of a different (set apart) community, and how he lives reflects upon it and upon the Head of that community. The Father's reputation is at stake.

If Your Counselee Argues

It is altogether likely that your counselee will argue with you. In such cases it is important to remember Who is the principal Counselor. It is the Holy Spirit, not you. You are but one who "ministers" His Word. To *minister* is "to serve." It is a term that was used of waiters. When a waiter serves food, he is not responsible for how rare or well done the meat may be, for its seasoning, and so on. He merely serves the meal. It is the cook who is the one who made the dish. And, if there is to be an appeal, it ought to be made to him. So too, it is God alone with Whom the resistant counselee must argue. Not with you. You simply serve the Word. The interesting fact is that God always prepares exactly what every believer needs at exactly the time when he needs it. He never makes a mistake. These facts need to be made abundantly clear to the counselee who persists on arguing: "You are not arguing with me; you are complaining against God."

Suppose You Get Nowhere

If after having explained the verses in I Peter and applied them to the counselee's case he fails to respond in faith, you may need to resort to church discipline. Now, you are not to move to this stage before you have tried every other means. It is only when the counselee is obstinate, determined to do as he wishes in the face of clear biblical commands to the contrary, that you must bring discipline against him. You have clearly shown him that you understand that what God wants may be difficult, that his faith may waver, but that God's will for him is always best. That fact is what you are anxious for him to accept by faith. Of course, you must believe this. But when church discipline is necessary, even then you must make it clear that this is for his benefit. Indeed, you will explain that church discipline is a privilege that God has accorded to His children that you have no right to withhold. It is intended to be a blessing to bring him back into fellowship with His Father and other members of His family.

What If A Counselee Leaves?

Since you will often find yourself dealing with the a counselee's tension between faith and desire, you must understand how to deal with it as Peter directs. Moreover, it is important to believe that God's way is best and that when you follow it, as a counselor you will honor Him and bless others. Even if your counselee refuses to obey God's Word (and often may leave in a huff because he didn't get his way), you must stand your ground. You must be certain, of course, that the ground on which you stand is entirely biblical. And you must also be sure that the counselee understands thoroughly what it is in Scripture that he is rejecting. Then, even if he leaves, if he repents later on, he will surely remember who it was who spoke the truth (hard as it may have been) to him. And often, it will be to you that he will return in the future when he needs help.

Now, be sure that your own faith is strong enough to overcome any desire *you* may have to fudge in these matters. Stand firm. Never allow a counselee to convince you to act out of accordance with God's will.

15

The Assurance of Faith

The "assurance of faith" refers that assurance which comes from, or arises out of, faith. This is important to recognize since there are many believers who are confused about the matter. You will encounter counselees who doubt their salvation. When you ask them, "Do you believe that Jesus Christ died for your sins?", they answer, "Certainly." But then, they go on to say, "But I'm not sure I am saved." This is a peculiar response, yet not infrequent. Were you to ask a counselee who his father is, he would tell you. And if you went on to ask whether he belonged to his father's family, again he'd answer, "Of course." But, why doesn't he see this in relationship to the heavenly Father and His children?

A Proper Focus is Crucial

There may be other reasons why some Christians find themselves perplexed about their salvation, but the principal one, it seems, is that they are basing their assurance upon their works. There is, of course, the general teaching that it is "by their works you shall know them." But this has to do with identifying true or false faith in another. Here, we are speaking about the assurance of one's personal faith that one has in him. The two must be distinguished—even though they often are not.

When we speak about the assurance that one has concerning his own salvation, we must focus not on works (though, in general, there will be some in the life of every true believer), but on his faith. What do I mean by that? Just what the writer to the Hebrews meant when he spoke of the "full assurance of hope" (Hebrews 6:11). Presumably, there were those who were becoming spiritually "dull"[1] (v. 12). Because the writer knew that the only thing that would give vitality to their lives would be assurance, he longed for them to show an "eagerness" for their faith that would persist "to the very end" (v. 11). He wanted them to know the joy of certainty that the promises of God were truly their inheritance. So, he spoke of the "assurance of hope." The "hope," of course, is the expectation that God will fulfill His "promises" that pertain to eternal life.

Assurance and Faith Inseparable

Now, this assurance is part and parcel of true faith. Think about it for a minute. When one says that he believes in Jesus Christ as His Savior, what does that mean? Naturally, it means many things, but central to all is the fact that the one making this confession of faith is saying "I trust that Jesus Christ will save me from all of my sins and take me to be with Him for eternity." If it doesn't mean that—or words to that effect—then what sort of faith is it?

Assurance is Normal

It is as normal for a Christian to have assurance as it is for a child to know that his father is his father. It is an abnormal condition for a child growing up in a loving home with his parents not to know that he is their child. Tell your counselee so. How absurd to think that God, the perfect Father, would keep His children guessing about their sonship. Even most poor human fathers wouldn't do that!

---

1 *Nothros*, the word used here, can mean sluggish, dull, or even comalike. It speaks of those who have lost the joy and certainty of the hope (expectation) of eternal life.

A Frequent Expression of the Problem

Here is what one such counseling conversation might look like.

Bob: "I am so worried about my salvation. I have great doubts from time to time about whether I am a child of God or not. Can you help me?"

Counselor: "If you are truly a believer, there is no reason why I can't. Let's talk about it."

Bob: "Good. I hope you can help. It's agony to lie awake at night wondering that if I don't awake here in this life I may awake in hell!"

Counselor: "Have you ever made a profession of faith in Christ?"

Bob: "Oh, yes. Several times. As a matter of fact, I keep on telling Him that I believe over and over again every day."

Counselor: "Well, don't you know that once is enough?"

Bob: "I know. But I'm never sure that I've really done it."

Counselor: "Let's examine what it means to believe in Christ. According to Romans 10:9, it means to confess with your mouth and believe in your heart that 'Jesus is Lord' and that 'God raised Him from the dead.' " And according to 1 Corinthians 15:3–4, Paul says that the gospel by which one is saved is: "Christ died for our sins in agreement with the Scriptures, and that He was buried, and that He was raised on the third day in agreement with the Scriptures. The question is: 'Do you believe those things and have you confessed Jesus as your Lord?' "

Bob: "I believed them from the first time that I heard them."

Counselor: "Then, if that's so, you are saved."

Bob: "But what if my faith is not genuine? Paul says that it is possible for one's faith to be 'empty' (1 Corinthians 15:2). That is, it's not genuine. What if I have 'empty' faith?"

Counselor: "Ah. You misunderstand that verse. What Paul says is not to be thought of as something that is actually possible. In this chapter, he is preparing for a discussion of the error of some in the Corinthian church who thought that there is no resurrection from the dead. He says that if there is no resurrection, clearly, Christ wasn't raised. Then, he says, 'If Christ hasn't been raised [from the dead], your faith is worthless; you are still in your sins' (1 Corinthians 15:17). But as he goes on to assert in the following verses, Christ has been raised from the dead and that faith in Him is not worthless (empty). He is not discussing the reality or falsehood of one's faith; his concern is whether or not *genuine faith* has been placed in a truth or a falsehood."

Bob: "Well, that helps explain one passage that has troubled me."

Counselor: Now, let's go back to what we were saying. The Bible teaches that all who believe the gospel are saved. Let me ask you again, 'Do you believe?' "

Bob: "Well, I try to believe, but I don't know ..."

Counselor: "You try to believe? What does that mean?"

Bob: "I'm not sure. I guess it means that I am making every effort to have genuine faith."

Counselor: "Does the Bible teach that salvation is based on your efforts or on what Christ did?"

Bob: "Well, … When you put it that way, I guess I have to say not on anything that I do, but only on what He did for me."

Counselor: "Good. You've got the heart of the matter straight. Salvation isn't based on what you do, only on what He did."

Bob: "Yes … but …"

Counselor: "Why should there be a 'but'?"

Bob: "Because I'm not sure about myself …"

Counselor: "There you go again, looking back at yourself. It is faith in Him—and what He did—that saves, not faith in one's self."

Bob: "I can see that. But what if I don't really have faith?"

Counselor: "Do you believe that Christ died for sinners like you? And that God raised Him from the dead thereby showing that He accepted His death as sufficient payment for their sins?"

Bob: "Certainly. There isn't any doubt about what He did. My only problem is about what I did—or didn't do."

Counselor: "OK. Let's examine that. Either you believe that God will do what He says He will do for all those who believe the gospel or you don't. He says He will save them. Right?"

Bob: "Right.

Counselor: "And you said that you believe it. Right?"

Bob: "Right."

Counselor: "If you do, then you are saved. The problem isn't your faith—as if you didn't have the right kind of faith or it is too weak. It is adequate—you believe!"

Bob: "Hmmmm …"

Counselor: "When you say that you believe the gospel, you are telling me that you have genuine faith. You have a hope (expectation) as a result. And that expectation is that God will give eternal life to all who believe. And you are one who does."

Bob: "I can see that, but …"

Bob: "Your doubt centers on yourself. And well it should if salvation in any way depended on you. Even your faith is not meritorious. It is but the instrument by which the gift of eternal life is received. What is it that God does for those who believe in Christ?"

Bob: "He saves them."

Counselor: "Are you sure?"

Bob: "There is no doubt about that!"

Counselor: "Then, if you believe that, you are saved. There is an assurance that goes along with true faith; it is the assurance that 'I am saved because God's promises don't fail.' It is that assurance of faith that grows out of God's promise that you have been having trouble with because you have been expecting assurance to come from what *you* do."

Bob: "I think I see it. My assurance doesn't arise from true faith itself but from God's promises that I believe."

Counselor: "You've got it! You see, faith is faith in God, not in yourself. You have been adding to faith in what God has done some idea of faith in your faith."

Now, not all doubts about salvation come from the problem discussed in this scenario. But many—perhaps most—do. It is imperative, then, for counselors to understand where the problem lies. In discussing the matter with counselees, what you are doing is helping them to come to "full assurance of hope" (Hebrews 6:11) so that, as the writer says, they will be eager "to the very end" to inherit God's promises (v. 12). It is assurance that arises out of that hope itself, "the full assurance of [that comes from] hope." The answer to the problem is understanding that Christ alone is our hope of eternal life and not our faith.

16

Is Faith Really Effective?

James wrote:

Is anybody among you sick? Let him call for the elders of the church and let them pray over him, rubbing him with oil in the Name of the Lord, and the believing prayer will deliver the one who is sick, and the Lord will raise him up. And if he has committed sins, he will be forgiven.

(5:14–15)

There are Christians who have a difficult time believing this promise. They ask such things as: "Is this always true? I prayed for my sick child and she only got worse and died. How can I believe?" Well, because you will be presented with this question sooner or later, you will need to have a ready, biblical answer.

A Number of Considerations

First, consider *all* that James says. Notice that he urges the sick one to call for the elders of his church. Too often people leave the matter to the grapevine: "Why doesn't the pastor come and see me?" The grapevine works all too well when relaying gossip, but when it is something urgent, it sometimes breaks down. The initiative does not belong to the pastor; it belongs to the sick person.

Note also that it is not the pastor of the congregation who is to be sent for; it is the elders of the church as a body. How many churches have even thought about this, let alone practiced it? I'm not talking about liberal churches, but Biblebelieving ones. When is the last time the elders were sent for in your congregation?

What About Anointing?

Then, there is the additional fact that they are to rub him with oil. The King James Version confused many by translating "rubbing him with oil" by "anointing him with oil." That isn't what the phrase says. The ceremonial term, from which the word "Christ" (*Chrio*) comes, means "to anoint." Jesus is the "Anointed One."[1] The person so anointed usually had oil poured on his head. Jesus was anointed with water at John's baptism, to appoint Him to His ministry. But the word James uses is *aleipho*. This is a very different word. It was used of rubbing down Greek athletes. Indeed, a noun form of the word meant "the massager." But of greater significance to us is the fact that the term was used by physicians to describe the rubbing of oil on the bodies of the sick. Various herbs (e.g., laurel seeds) were mixed in oil as the medium and smeared and rubbed on the sick. So, rather than ordain a ceremony with a ceremonial rite, James was talking about using medicine.

Since doctors were not to be found on every corner, and because they had no corner on the practice of medicine, much medical work was done by laymen. Here, the elders are told to use medicinal means to heal along with prayer.

"But what about that prayer of faith?" your counselee may ask. Let's look at that as well. First, it was to be offered in faith. That's crucial. Remember that, in speaking about a doubter, James said, "That person shouldn't suppose that he will receive anything from the Lord" (1:7). So, the prayer of the elders must be a believing one. "Is the sick person to pray in faith too?" While he is not specifically mentioned, the answer must be, "Of course." It is clear that, unlike many, he believed the Bible enough to send for the elders in the

---

1   As the Greek word *christos* means "the Anointed One," so too does the Hebrew *mesheach* from which "Messiah" is derived.

first place. It is hardly true that he would have done so without thinking that this is how God would answer his prayer for healing.

Confession of Sin

Then in addition, notice that if the sickness is in any way due to one's sin, he is to confess it to the one whom he has wronged (v. 16) and God will forgive him. There are at least two ways in which sin might contribute to illness. A person by sinning may injure himself (for example, in a drunken brawl). Or the sickness may be a divine judgment (cf. 1 Corinthians 11:20, 27–30) because of sin. The passage does not specify which of these is in view. So it must be construed as referring to both possibilities. After all, no matter what its origin may be, sin must be confessed and forgiven (v. 16). While all sickness isn't attributable to an individual's sin, unless it is evident that the sickness is, it is important for the elders to raise the matter with the sick person. They are not to presuppose that the one who is ill has brought it on himself, however, but merely to inquire about the possibility. Now, until all of the above conditions are met, it is foolish to think that God has not kept His promise to raise the sick person up from his sick bed.[2]

A Failed Promise?

"OK," your counselee may say. "But suppose all of the conditions are met. Does God always keep His promise to raise the sick?" Well, of course, God always keeps His promise. There are numerous occasions when, not following the directions given in James 5, people complain that God has failed to respond to their prayers. Ask, "Did the sick person summon the elders?" Did they come? Did they pray in faith? Did they encourage the person to employ the best medical treatment possible? Were sins

2 James is not talking about every minor injury or illness (colds, etc.) but those that are serious enough to bring about a bedridden condition (the words, "pray over him" indicate that he is on a sick bed).

confessed and forgiven, if necessary?" All of these questions should be answered in the affirmative before one begins to wonder about God keeping His promises. There are human responsibilities to be fulfilled. In the largest number of cases, there is good reason to suspect that the sick person (or his family) as well as the elders have failed in assuming their responsibilities. When God has set forth a procedure that He follows, man must get involved in it. It is not up to us to tell God that we have a better idea.

But there are times when God does not answer the prayer of the believer and his church—even when it is offered in faith. "Ah! So He doesn't always keep His promises." That is the wrong conclusion to reach. While James sets a rule for the ordinary situation, there are exceptions. The time for God to take the sick Christian to Himself may have arrived. Clearly, the promise wasn't intended to be applied to such situations or no sick Christians who followed James' directions would ever die from an illness!

Are there other exceptions? Certainly. God has His purposes in not healing every affliction. Paul prayed three times before realizing that his was one of those exceptional cases. He had a physical affliction (probably having to do with his eyesight) that God refused to relieve him of—for his own benefit (cf. 2 Corinthians 12:1–10). God had taken Paul to heaven and given him such marvelous revelations that he might have become proud. The affliction was continued to keep him humble.

Now, God might not have that particular purpose in view in allowing the sick person to remain in his illness. But He may do so for some other good purpose. True faith is willing to accept the exception! Moreover, one must not give up. The passage does not say how long it will take for the sick person to be healed of his illness. If unbelief creeps in and people become unwilling to conform to God's timing, they may miss the blessing that they could have had by enduring (cf. James 1:2–4). The passage doesn't speak about instantaneous, miraculous healing. Indeed, the fact that medicine is also to be applied indicates that it is a more ordinary cure that is in view. So, while James give us a general rule concerning sickness, it is not to be understood as absolute. All he says is that if the person is to be healed of a serious illness by God, this is how it is to be accomplished. The way described gives all of the glory to God, but also assures us of the propriety of using medicinal means for healing.

17

Conclusion

In this book, I have covered the nature of faith, its importance to counseling, and several of the complications with reference to it that a counselor might meet in the course of counseling sessions. I have attempted to give clear, biblical advice about how to handle these and guidance in how to encourage faith in counselees.

We have seen that "without faith it is impossible to please" God (Heb. 11:6). That, of course, is why faith is so important. It is the chief factor in the discussion that I have sought to stress. Whether or not a counselee pleases God as the result of changing through faith in God's Word and Spirit is of prime concern. As a goal, it ranks above every other. The welfare of the counselee depends upon faith. When there are results in solving problems, they are but a by-product of acting in faith. Trusting God throughout counseling is uppermost.

Faith that pleases God is uppermost not only for the counselee, but also for the counselor. I have shown how lack of faith on his part, though not inevitably, can bring about failure. Often, such failure to trust God's promises can even cause greater harm to counselees. So, the importance of faith in all that is done in counseling is clear.

Now, far too much counseling is done without a thought or mention of the important place of faith. That is the main reason I have written—to urge counselors to emphasize faith's role in counseling. I hope to remind counselors of these known, doctrinal facts that are so easily forgotten in the routine of work.

Whatever your situation, I trust that this look at faith in relationship to counseling has so encouraged biblical counselors that it will result in much more faithful counseling in the church of Christ, counseling that will please Jesus Christ. After all, the entire work of counseling, like the actual process of doing it, should be done for the biblical purpose of bringing God's people in conformity to His Son, all to the glory of God. To be well-pleasing to Him is the final end of the Christian's life and, therefore, extends to all that a believer does in life.

Christian counselor, think about faith in counseling as you prepare for counseling cases, as you enter the counseling room, as you give counsel to those to whom you minister. And as you correct and direct counselees toward biblical behavior be sure that you stress faith as a prominent topic. The importance of faith in counseling should permeate your counseling.

There is little more to say; now is the time for application rather than additional discussion. Just remember, emphasizing faith in counseling focuses everyone's attention on pleasing God. That is how it should be.